Making Your Life Simply Simple

by

Richard Flint

*6 Steps To Achieving The Simplicity
You Keep Talking About Wanting For Your Life*

❝ Making Your Life Simply Simple is a very enjoyable quick read. There are so many tidbits of practical information contained that makes it a must read. ❞

— **Dr. Charlie Sink, Owner, Grand Paws Animal Clinic**

❝ The title of the book, Making Your Life Simply Simple brings purely comforting feelings. Reading the book, however, makes it clear that improving one's life is both simple and complex. The challenge lies in thoroughly reading, digesting and implementing the advice. ❞

— **Samantha Ley, Wife, Mother, Real Estate Investor**

❝ Richard Flint's book, Making Your Life Simply Simple is a must read! This book digs down into the things we all know are true about ourselves and is able to help shed light on the pathway to making lasting improvements. The steps outlined are what we all need to finally achieve the simple life we all desire. ❞

— **Jeff Ley, Real Estate Investor**

❝ By the time I got to the actual '6 Steps To Making Your Life Simply Simple' I was reminded of all the frustration and waste of years and relationships in my life, but really thought that at my age I had worked it all out. Then, reading the steps – when I came to the 5th Step, I was moved that I have one more thing to do, and it was found in that chapter. How can simplicity sound so easy and be so difficult? ❞

— **Bob McKinnon, Director of Leadership, Exit Realty Corp. International**

❝ Simply Simple is a key to have a life of purpose. It's a code of ethic to guide us to believe in ourselves, to set realistic goals, take appropriate actions and celebrate success along the journey. As I was reading, it was like a handbook to the coaching you have provided my life. <u>Making Your Life Simply Simple</u> can help others to make choices to climb out of the well to have a Simply Great Day Everyday. ❞

— **Robert (Bobby) L. Cutchins II, Founder/CVO, Bobby's Tire & Auto Care**

❝ It has been said, "When the student is ready, the teacher will appear." Well, such is the case with Richard's new book, <u>Making Your Life Simply Simple</u>. It could have not come along at a more appropriate time in my life. Richard will guide you on a journey toward clarity and certainty and away from the chaos and confusion in a way only Richard can do. ❞

— **Dr. Albert E Andrion, II, Andrion Chiropractic**

❝ I have known Richard Flint for many years, and am a big fan of his positive approach to life. I have read many of his books, and I always take away helpful life lessons. <u>Making Your Life Simply Simple</u> has hit home and has been of special significance in my life, especially after a couple of difficult years. I recommend that you read it. It will challenge your life and give you the tools to make every new day your best! ❞

— **Gene Paul Stifer, GM/COO, Palm Beach Bath and Tennis Club**

❝ What you remind me of so eloquently throughout this book is that it's simply a choice, and I still have time to make the right choices. Thanks again for the great advice and sage wisdom. ❞

— **Hunter Fennell, President, Seed, Inc.**

❝ The thought of making your life Simply Simple has such great appeal. As usual you have broken that concept down into clear and concise steps. <u>Making Your Life Simply Simple</u> is really a necessary part of our ongoing journey of life. Your book does a wonderful job of outlining the process. ❞

— **Dr. Ted Gehrig, DDS**

❝ Of all your books, this one I enjoyed the most. You don't waste time getting to the point, and you offer solutions for growth and improvement all the way through the book. ❞

— **Dennis Poulin, Owner, R&G Vent Cleaning**

❝ When Richard first told me that I needed to simplify my life, I nearly laughed out loud. To say I was skeptical would be a major understatement. Over time, one decision at a time, I came to realize the wisdom of his words and concepts. One day I looked around and realized I was actually HAPPY. Keeping it SIMPLE was the key. ❞

— **Doug Rogers, Owner, Autohaus Import Services**

❝ In a society so accustomed to living and working in chaos and confusion, it's refreshing to read a book about living a simpler existence. Richard Flint helps you remember that the choices we make, dictate the life we choose to lead. This book lays the groundwork for determining the path to a simpler, less stressful life; through calmness and trust in yourself. ❞

— **Gina Calla, Director of Human Resources, Sailfish Point**

Published 2017
Copyright 2017

ISBN# 978-0-937851-49-4
Flint, Inc. Product #3019

Printed in the United States of America.
For information write to
Richard Flint Seminars
11835 Canon Blvd., Suite B-108
Newport News, VA 23606-2570
or call 1-800-368-8255

www.RichardFlint.com

Cover Design by Denise Harden

All rights reserved. No part of this book may be reproduced in any form or by any electronic or mechanical means, including information storage or retrieval systems, without permission in writing from Flint, Inc., except by a reviewer, who may quote brief passages in a review.

Dedication

Dedicated to Doug Rogers whose realization that simple was possible challenged his thinking, redesigned his thinking and allowed him to step out of his rat race and make his life Simply Simple!

TABLE OF CONTENTS

Preface
The Choice Is Yours .... *i*

Chapter 1
The Simple Truth *1*

Chapter 2
Life's Simple Question *17*

Chapter 3
You Can Really Make a Mess Out of Your Life *23*

Chapter 4
Why Would You Choose To Mess Up Your Life *31*

Chapter 5
6 Steps To Making Your Life Simply Simple *43*

Chapter 6
Step 1: Start With Facing Where Your Life Is Right Now *47*

Chapter 7
Step 2: Invest Your Time In Cleaning Up The Clutter In Your Life *53*

Chapter 8
Step 3: Make Time For Yourself *57*

Chapter 9
Step 4: Pause When You Feel Your Life Is Becoming Overwhelmed ... *65*

Chapter 10
Step 5: Let Go of The Wrongs of Yesterday *71*

Chapter 11
Step 6: Enter Every Day Prepared To Have a Simply Great Day *77*

Conclusion
It's All In Your Hands *83*

Preface

The Choice Is Yours

*Life provides you with many paths to travel; each path creates a direction. **When you are traveling the path of simplicity, you get the rewards that go with Keeping Your Life Simply Simple!***

Living in the fast lane is not all it's built up to be. For some reason many believe the faster they move the more they are going to achieve. The *Simple Truth* is just the opposite. The greater control you have of your life the *simpler* your life becomes.

Alan put it this way, "Richard, I want it all! I want all life has to offer, and I want it right now. Why should I have to wait? I am committed to doing whatever it takes at whatever cost. I just want it all NOW!"

Dot said this to me, "Richard, I understand what you are saying about the need to slow my life down, but that is so foreign to me. I have never lived that way. I have not been trained to slow down. Every mentor, boss I have had has been about doing as much as you can as fast as you can. The message is *life is short and there may not be a tomorrow. So, grab it all now!* I have accepted that, and it has become the way I live. I know you are right, but I am not sure I can recreate whom I have become."

Do you know any Allen's or Dot's? They are not the extreme; they are actually the norm. It is so challenging for people to understand that *simple isn't a race; it is a journey.* Creating the *Simple Life* is not something that happens when you snap your fingers or click your heels. It's a journey that has to become a mindset you bring to your life each day and design a life that is about *Keeping Things Simply Simple!*

Do you understand what I mean when I say, "It is easier to live in confusion than it is to live in clarity?" Confusion is the norm; clarity is the exception. You are taught throughout your life to live in confusion. Life becomes about how much YOU can get done, how much YOU can have, how many things YOU can juggle at one time. The challenge is all these teachings are about YOU living out of control. They are about YOU moving faster than YOU can manage.

Then, one day YOU wake up and realize that all the fast pace has gotten you is tiredness, frustrations, disappointment and an inner anger toward what your life isn't. Now, you look at your life and talk about all the years you have wasted and felt overwhelmed, because you feel you have spent more time working against yourself than you have creating the life you really wanted, but never gave yourself permission to design. After all, *the people who stand outside your life with opinions know more about what is right for you than you do.* So, what do you do? You hand your life over to them and listen to what they feel you should be doing. In doing that you give up your design, your individuality and become a clone to what they feel you should be.

Have you ever watched parents do that to their kids? Have you ever bought into the concept that *the faster you move the more you are going to achieve?*

Mark is so talented when it comes to playing golf. There is no doubt he could make the PGA tour. He has a love hate relationship with the game. One day he asked if I would play a round of golf with him. I knew what was on his agenda, and I had wanted the opportunity to talk to him.

PREFACE

As we went around the course, he finally felt comfortable enough to talk to me about what I knew was troubling him.

As we were driving between holes, he stopped the cart and asked a question without looking at me. "Richard, what do you think of my dad?"

"Well, he is a very interesting personality. He sure wants you to make it in golf."

"You're right, but I think he wants it for him, not for me. He has always had this dream of making the tour. He is good, but deep down I think he knew he wasn't that good. I think I am the pathway he never got to walk."

"Why do you feel that way?"

"The pressure he puts on me. He pushes and pushes and says it is because he wants the best for me. I think part of that is true, but the biggest part is he wants it for his ego. To be honest with you, he is slowly sucking the fun out of the game for me. When he is at a tournament where I am playing, I can see him out of the corner of my eye, and I see all those facial expressions I know are saying 'disappointment.' I know when he thinks I have messed up, and it just eats at my insides. I want to tell him not to come, but he is paying for me to do this. I think I owe it to him. What can I do? Would you talk to him for me?"

"Mark, I can't do that. This is your challenge, and you have to handle it. I agree he has a hidden agenda. It's so apparent that he wants this for you, and at the same time he wants it for himself. He really is living through you."

Right now Mark is not playing golf. He became so frustrated with what was happening, he walked away. His dad is angry with him. He can't understand what happened. Both of their lives exist in confusion. His dad's desire for Mark to "do it" overshadowed Mark's desire to just play golf and make it a game, not a time of torture. Mark's dream became his nightmare. The *Simple Life* of playing a game he loved so much was eroded by his dad's pressure for Mark to *make it big*.

Everyday in all types of relationships the *Simple Life* is taken from people by the pressure that comes from allowing the outside to bring to their life. When overwhelming pressure overshadows your design and desire for your life, clarity is replaced with confusion. The result is the *simply simple becomes simply confusing*.

Your LIFE really is a choice you make everyday. It is not something that is just "handed" to you or something that just "happens" to you. Sure you are "handed" events, but with each event you get to make a choice. Sure, things are going to "happen" to you, but you still have a choice.

The choice you make creates the pathway you will travel. The pathway of choice creates the pathways to your life. This is why it is so important you understand, accept and implement choices that make your life *Simply Simple*. This is why it is imperative you make this *Simple Question* your guiding force in all your decision making:

Is this decision going to feed my confusion or strengthen my clarity?

This question is important to all aspects of your life and is why I will keep bringing it back for you to face. This is so much more than a question. This is a compass for living! It is the control panel to where you will go, what you will experience and the results your life will be handed.

Everyday you make choices! Those choices point your life toward:

- C   CONFUSION OR CLARITY
- H   HAVOC OR HAPPINESS
- O   OBSTACLES OR OPPORTUNITIES
- I   INTERRUPTIONS OR INVESTMENTS
- C   CLUTTER OR COMPLETION
- E   ESCAPE OR EVOLVING
- S   SENSELESS OR SENSIBLE LIVING

With each choice comes the life you create. Life is all about the decisions you make, which takes you in the direction the choice creates. It goes back to one of my *Simple Foundational Truths – You are perfectly designed to achieve what you are achieving!* There is no one or nothing to blame except you for what your life isn't! Your life is the by-product of the choices you make. The right choices make your life *Simply Simple!*

In the next chapters we are going to explore the meaning to **Making Your Life Simply Simple!** The Simple Truth is the *Simpler your life, the Simpler your life becomes.*

Making Your Life Simply Simple

Chapter 1

The Simple Truth

The Truth is always present, but not always wanting to be heard.

1

Art was an interesting person. He had called me several times to inquire about my Private Coaching. Each time he would listen to what was involved and tell me, "I need to think about this. Can I get back to you?"

My response was always, "Sure. Let me know when you are ready to talk more about the program." With that the conversation would end.

A few months ago I was speaking in Orlando and who was there? Art! I saw him coming and recognized that look on his face. It was one of question mixed with fear.

"Art, how are you?"

"I'm doing okay. Do you have a few moments to talk to me?"

"Come on; let's find a quiet place to talk.

We walked around the corner, found a couple of chairs and sat down. I just waited for him to begin.

"You know I have talked to you a couple of times about your Private Coaching program."

"Yes; I think we have talked three times and each time we left it with you will get back to me."

"I want to first apologize to you for taking your time. I was and am really interested in your Coaching Program. I get excited about working with you and then, my fear takes over. You scare the daylights out of me."

"Why? Why do I scare you?"

"Because you are you. You seem to be very direct, play no games and hold people accountable. I am not used to that level of truth. I live in a world where I fudge the truth. I know what it is, but I choose to redefine it in my favor. I know that's not being truthful, but it has been how I have lived my life and continue to live that way."

"And, what has living that way gotten you?"

There was this slight laugh, a smile and then, a look of pain. "It has just gotten me more pain. Richard, I am so tired! I am tired of my life and REALLY tired of me. I want out of this draining circle I have created for myself. I REALLY want out! I know you can help me, but I am fearful of facing myself, of facing the truth about me!"

Have you ever been there? Have you ever been ready to face your life, to face you and just been too fearful to do it?

The *Simple Truth* is *there is no possibility of growth in your life until you are willing to face yourself with the Truth About You!* That is one of the most challenging points people have to get to.

Truth is so simple, yet so complex!

One night when I was in a counseling session with Sandy, she put it this way. "Richard, I am not dumb! I know me better than anyone. I sit here, talk to you and think *I know this.* I know what I need to do, but I still don't do it. I talk to myself and have some challenging conversations about my behavior and realize my behavior is contradicted by my actions. To use your words, *Behavior Never Lies.* My life is really not complicated. I just choose to make it that way. Truth is, I know what to do; I just don't do it. That makes the simple you talk about so complex!"

Sandy is so right! I have seldom ever sat with a person who didn't know what they needed to do with their life. They knew the truth; that part was simple. What they couldn't do was take the Truth and implement it into the actions necessary to calm their life and take them out of their Circle of Sameness.

Why is the *Simple Truth* so challenging for so many? From my years of working with the human personality let me share with you the most consistent challenges the Truth presents that make it complex.

First, *the Truth is frightening!* It requires you take an HONEST look at your behavior and face what it says about you. This means looking at yourself from the inside – out, rather than the outside – in.

The difference is outside – in is based on living through the opinions of others. You let them define your life; you give them permission to own you emotionally. With that design you don't have to face yourself; you can hide behind what others are saying. The Truth about you gets buried under the opinions of others.

When you live from the inside – out, there is no escaping YOU! Alone with you, YOU have to be honest. You have to be truthful about YOU. Can you sense, feel the fright that might create in some people? When you can't hide from yourself, there will be fear involved in the journey.

Ray was one of these outside-in people. He came to me at a point where he was really down on himself. His opening words to me were, "I am so tired of being me!" There was a pause followed by these words, "No, that isn't true! I am tired of being what everyone else tells me I need to be. I have lost me! Richard, I want out of the vicious circle. I want to discover whom I am and have the life that goes with that."

"Ray, what do you think that is going to require?"

"I am going to have to stop letting others control me, look at myself with an honest eye, and be willing to learn whom I am."

"With all the years of letting others control you, do you think that will be easy?"

"Easy!! I am not even sure I can do it, but I want out of

the draining life I have created by giving others the right to tell me whom I am. Can you help me?"

It wasn't easy for Ray. There were times he told me, "I can't do this! I am not strong enough to face me, be honest about me, to make the changes I have to make."

It took almost two years of hard work for Ray, but he did it! He moved from being an outside-in person to living his life from the inside-out. I saw him recently, and when he saw me, he ran over, gave me a big hug and said in a smiling voice, "Thank You! I have never been so happy with me. I now have my life, and I am enjoying it. You said life could be simpler when I learned to trust and believe in me, and it has! I love being me!"

Facing yourself can be very frightening. Why? You spend more time listening to others and giving them permission to define whom you are, than you do trusting yourself and allowing yourself to be you.

The second reason the *Simple Truth* is so challenging is *it refuses to lie!* Most would tell you they don't lie, but anytime you *refuse* to face the Truth, a lie is involved. A lie is any pathway that takes you away from the reality of what is actually happening.

Matt said this to me. "Richard, I don't lie. I just don't deal with what I need to deal with. How can that be a lie?"

It's a "lie" because it is not dealing with the Truth of "what is." Until you are willing to face your life with Total Honesty, you have to lie to yourself. The opposite of a lie is the Truth! That's the Truth!

If you are going to stretch for the Simple Life, you have to face yourself with honesty. Every time there is any point of contradiction, there is confusion. Confusion takes away the possibility of having a Simple Life.

Patty is such an interesting person, yet she is one complex human. She came to me wanting me to mentor her and ask, "What does it take to become one of your mentoring students?"

"You have to be ready for me!"

"What does that mean?"

"You have to be willing to face yourself and be willing to not be fearful to peel the onion layers back and get to the core of your life. You have got to have a desire to go forward that is stronger than your fear of facing yourself.":

"You mean you have to get honest with yourself."

"Patty, that is the essence of what my mentoring is about. You can't go beyond what you are willing to face. So many talk about what they want, but implement behavior that makes that impossible. They spend more time strengthening their confusion than they do working to improve their life. Until you are ready to face yourself, you can't move toward making your life simple. Are you ready for that journey?"

"To be honest with you, I am not sure. I live with the fear of the unknown. I have created this life for myself, and I am not sure I want to disturb it. It is not all that bad."

"Is it the life you really want?"

"No, but it is not all that bad."

Patty was not ready for me. Since that conversation, I have not heard from her, but I have heard that her life is more confusing now than ever. Until you are ready to face the truth about you, YOU are not ready to achieve a Simple Life.

The third reason the *Simple Truth* is so challenging for many people is it *uncovers what you are and have been running from.* I wish people really understood the Truth to my statement, "Anything you think you are running from, you are actually running toward."

You can't escape the Truth! You can run, but you can't hide from the Truth; you can avoid, but you can't deny the Truth; you can look the other way, but the truth will still be there beside you.

Paul came to me from a recommendation from a mutual friend. The friend knew Paul and knew the mess he had gotten his life in. I met Paul at Panera Bread, and I could tell by looking at him he was nervous and not sure about why he was there.

"Richard, Jason said I needed to meet with you. I don't know what we are going to talk about, but he told me *if there is anyone who can help you get out of this mess you have created for yourself and get your life on a simpler path, it is Richard.* So, I am here!"

As we talked, it was apparent that Paul had created this path where he was running away from most everything in his life. He lived with enormous fear and denial.

"Paul, why are you running away from facing yourself?"

"The truth! I don't like me. I can't tell you a time I have ever liked whom I am or what I am. I have been living this life of avoiding, lying and running, I don't know any other way to live."

"Do you enjoy living this way?"

"NO! I am angry, tired and just wish this life was over. I am not happy; I have no joy in my life; I feel lost every single day of my life. This life is a living hell!"

Paul and I spent the next year working on finding the REAL Paul and learning how to not allow this dangerous Paul from having control of his life. I get emails from him and he tells me how much he is enjoying his life today. He was able to be honest with himself and face his yesterday that was designed to hold him hostage.

You can spend your entire life running from the "who" you see yourself as or you can face your life and discover "whom" you can become. There is no "Simple" in running from yourself.

Another of the *Simple Truths* I have learned is *most seek to avoid, rather than confront the Truths they know about their self.* This means each day they have designed a pathway away from improving their life and are collecting more emotional garbage they will have to face.

Alexia is a bright, caring person who has a great personality. She is a social butterfly whom everyone loves being around. She is always the life of the party. If you looked at her, you would think she was one of the most all together people you have ever met. Yet, when you get to the Alexia that lives behind the social butterfly mask, you find a very frightened and lonely person.

I met her on an airplane flying back into Palm Beach. We had struck up a conversation on the flight. Toward the end of the flight, she looked at me with a very serious look and said, "Where have you been? I have needed someone like you for years. Richard, I am so tired of pretending. I live in this fake world where I am not me. I wear this mask so people can't get to know me. If they really got to know me, they wouldn't want to be around me."

It happened that she lived very close to me, so I agreed to meet with her. Those meetings lasted for almost six months. The #1 thing we worked on was Alexia's fear of confronting herself. She had come from a very negative and destructive background that had created a script of low self-esteem and a life of denial, which became her path of escape. Slowly, we were able to rewrite the scripts she had been programmed with and free her from the falsehoods she had been living.

The last time I saw her, her words to me were, "I love this life I now have. I am free to be me. I don't have to pretend anymore. You know, when you love who you are, it makes life so much easier!"

Making your life simple is really simple, but at the same time complex. You have got to be willing to confront your view of yourself and not be afraid to be honest about YOU!

Truth is revealing and for many that is not fun! For most when looking at their life is not fun, they will create a pathway to avoid confronting what they need to address.

The next reason the *Simple Truth* is so challenging for many people is it *takes courage to implement*. Most are not cowards; they are *simply* grounded in so much fear it holds them hostage.

You must never forget "Courage is not the absence of fear; it is the inner strength to act in spite of it!" There will always be fear in your life! The other aspect of this fact is that fear doesn't have to own you emotionally. Don't ever forget *– fear never travels by itself!* All emotions travel in threes. When fear is present, so is doubt, worry and uncertainty. Put these three together, and they will paralyze you. When you are paralyzed, you just keep adding more and more layers of confusion to your life.

It takes courage to face yourself with honesty; it takes courage to look at yourself in life's mirror and be honest about your behavior.

Sarah said this to me. "I am the person you keep talking about. I am paralyzed, but only because I don't want to face me! I know that; I keep telling myself I am going to stop doing this, but know what? I don't. I am so tired of living in this maze. I want out and yes, I know the first step is facing me." It takes such a strong desire to be willing to face yourself. Look back over the people we have looked at and learn one lesson. Confusion makes your life an emotional mess. Confusion steals the Simple! I know this is challenging to understand, *but making your life Simply Simple is simply making choices that take you forward through truth.*

The last reason the *Simple Truth* is so challenging for many people is you *have to commit to doing it.*

Last night I had a phone call from Michele. This was our fourth call in four nights. She was struggling with the direction for her life. Her dream has her looking in one direction and her fear looking in another. I've known her for four years and her challenge has been the same. I finally told her, "I am tired of these circle conversations. Michele, you can't continue to walk this fence! It is wearing on you, and what I see is you are moving further and further away from the pathway you really want."

I paused, raised the pitch of my voice and said with force, "If you aren't going to do anything, then, stop talking about what you are going to do. You are not being honest with me or yourself. I don't want to hear it anymore."

I wish you could have heard the silence on the other end of the phone. I could here her breathing increase and the emotions being expressed. "You are right! I know you are right. I need to settle this fear inside me. I really know what I want, but I am so fearful. I don't trust myself. I keep replaying all those old tapes from my mom and dad about how I will never be able to do anything in my life. My dream would mean stepping out on my own, trusting in my talents and letting go of those people who are using me. I know all this! I just need to DO IT! Why am I so afraid?"

Michele is like so many. She has the sketch of what she wants for her life, but stops short of committing her self to doing it. The *Simple Truth* is *there will be no growth in her life until she is willing to commit, face her fear and act in spite of it!*

Life really is simple, but it is not always easy! It just takes getting out of your own way and living with *Simple Truths*. Let me give you six (6) *Simple Truths* for preparing your life for growth.

Truth #1: Stay Centered So You Can Maintain Balance!

The more scattered your life becomes the more confusion you will wrestle with. Confusion creates the fear, the doubt, the worry, the uncertainty that makes the detours look attractive. Remember, all of these are emotions and when they are in control, all you can make are emotional decisions. It's your emotions that see the detour, not your imagination.

Stay Centered on making your life calm. Before you say "YES!" to anything put it to the ***Simplicity Question – will this feed my confusion or strengthen my clarity?*** It is the question that will keep you pointed toward a Simple life.

> **Truth #2: Invest In Your Mind In Order To Control Your Emotions!**

If you don't have a daily process of feeding your mind, you spend each day strengthening your emotions. Either your mind or your emotions are designing the pathway for a day of your life.

The question is, *How dangerous are you when you are running purely on emotions?* You know the answer to that question! When you are running purely on your emotions, you take the "Simple" out of the equation. You make the simple complex!

Invest in your mental clarity. Make sure each morning you begin your day with a diet of mental focus and mental clarity. This is why I created my Morning Minute. Each morning you receive in your email in-box a 1 minute video email from me with a thought to start your day with and points of wisdom to nibble on all day. The Morning Minute is mental fiber you can feast on all day.

> **Truth #3: Manage Your Pace, So Your Pace Doesn't Manage You!**

I believe PACE is one of the internal strengths you need to manage to have growth in your life. When I say "Pace," I am not talking about physical speed. I am talking about mental and emotional control.

The faster you move emotionally, the more reactions you are going to bring to your life. The faster you are moving emotionally the more opportunities you run by and miss the growth they offer your life.

The more control you give your mind, the easier it is for you to respond with clarity and calmness. When these two unite, they turn your imagination lose to see the BIG picture of what is there for your life. Hey, the clearer the picture, the Simpler it is for you to achieve your desired success.

> **Truth #4: Protect Yourself From Those Who Want To Steal Your Spirit!**

The more you want to do with your life the fewer people you can have in your life. For years I have taught a very *Simple, but Complex* truth – *don't keep anyone in your life who is not part of your fan club!* So many who stand in your life are not there to support or even help you with your growth. Many times their negativity stands between you and your dream. They are jealous, envious or fearful of your growth. You can't change them! Again, that is more than words; it is a fact. The more control you give them the more attention you pay them. That attention only strengthens their presence. You must confront their behavior, challenge them to improve and let them know they will not remain in your life if they continue to be your critic.

Don't be sucked in by their words, "I am only trying to help you." That is not true! Those who support you, challenge you with a spirit that says, "I care." Those who attack you stand in your life with a critical approach that is based in "what you can't do," or "how you are doing it is wrong."

You need positive energy for growth. Each time you fight with a negative person they steal positive energy from you; this leaves you emotionally drained, mentally off track and spiritually down. The only way to protect yourself is being willing to confront and eliminate negative people.

The Simple Truth is negative people don't care about you! They want to hold you an emotional hostage to their agenda.

Truth #5: Learn From Yesterday; Don't Relive It!

Yesterday is a reference library, not a room to live in! That is a *Simple Truth* many have never learned. Without this understanding an unfulfilled life keeps standing in yesterday talking about what their life hasn't been, rehashing why it hasn't happened and blaming the universe for the state of being.

Reality is, *yesterday is a vital part of your growth, WHEN it is used correctly.* Yesterday contains a vault of successes for you to draw from. Learning happens when you find the lesson, apply it to your today and implement improvement that keeps pushing you forward.

You can't stand in yesterday and have a today that is better! You must stand in today, draw from what you learned from yesterday and use it to have a consistent journey of personal growth. A better tomorrow is the result of a today that used yesterday to gain understanding, courage and appreciation for what their life had been handed.

Truth #6: Everything Is Your Choice; Make Wise Decisions!

This truth is *Simple, but frightening*. It simply says *I am perfectly designed to achieve what I am achieving.* You are today the result of the choices you have made up to this point. With everything your life is handed there is a choice attached.

Those choices are about:
- chaos or calmness
- havoc or healthy decisions
- obstacles or opportunities
- inconsistencies or investments
- confusion or clarity
- emotionally reacting or mentally responding.

In essence that is your life! You choose, and then you receive the pathway your choice creates. It really has nothing to do with what life has brought your way; it is all about what you have chosen to do with the event.

If you really want to know the *Simple Truth*, you are standing in a today that is the result of the choices you have made. If you don't like where your choices are taking you, wise up and make choices that are designed to *strengthen your clarity, not feed your confusion!*

It really is that SIMPLE!!! The *Simple Truth* is *there is no possibility of growth in your life until you are willing to face yourself with Truth About You!*

Simple Keys To Learn About The Choices You Make:

C   CALMNESS MUST GUIDE YOUR DECISION

H   HAVE TRUST IN YOURSELF

O   OPEN YOURSELF TO LISTENING TO THOSE INNER WHISPERS

I   INVEST IN GETTING TO REALLY KNOW YOURSELF

C   CREATE YOUR LIFE; DON'T LET OTHERS DO IT FOR YOU

E   EXTRACT LESSONS AND IMPLEMENT THEM

S   STAY TRUE TO YOURSELF

Chapter 2

Life's Simple Question

When you know what questions to ask, life becomes so much simpler.

I finished the program I was doing and walked outside the room. I was putting things in my computer bag when I looked up and saw him standing there just staring at me. I paused, looked at him and said, "How are you?"

There was a moment of silence and this reply, "I just finished listening to you, and I don't agree with the principle you were sharing."

With that there was a pause and a look that appeared to be waiting for me to say something. I smiled and said, "I covered several principles I believe. Which one are you referring to?"

"The one about life being simple. I don't agree with that. Do I want a simple life? Yes! Do I think it is possible? No! There is just too much junk for life to be simple."

I stopped fiddling with my bag and asked, "You don't think it is possible to have a simple life?"

"NO!"

I took a step toward him, looked him squarely in the eyes and said, "Is it possible, just possible that I am right, and the reality is you can't see it, because you have made your life too complex?"

The look on his face told me he wasn't sure what to say. Here is the interesting thing. I have had that same conversation with hundreds of people. I have found the two things most people are seeking is simplicity and stability. They talk about having that life, but design their life for confusion.

Life really is a choice! Each day is given to you, BUT you get to decide what you do with it. A "bad day" is a day you chose to have a "bad day!" A "good day" is a day you chose to have a "good day." The difference between the two is not the events the day brought, but what you choose to do with the events of the day.

Do you understand most days don't begin with you getting up in the morning; they begin with how you went to bed the night before. If you go to bed frustrated, upset or even angry, you will get up the next morning with these same emotions residing inside you. You can, and many do, carry emotional residue from one day to the next.

The majority of people don't emotionally clean out their life before they go to bed. How many times have you heard, "All I need is a good night's sleep, and things will be better in the morning." The reality is, they are not! What you carry over from day to day just increased its internal presence in your life. Carry stuff over long enough, and you will begin to think "this is the way my life is going to be." If and when that attitude sets in, you are guaranteed to have a streak of "bad days."

I believe we were not put on this earth to have "bad days." Granted, not each day is going to be your "best day," but if you understand The Simple Truth a "bad day" simply becomes a challenging day.

Making Simple, Simple is really simple, but at the same time complex. Now, I know that sounds like double talk, but it's not. For any Truth to bring strength to your life, it has to have a consistent persistency in your life. In working with human behavior here is how I have found the majority of people approach life. They are looking for instant gratification, instant results, instant rewards. When that doesn't happen, they approach their life with the attitude, "I knew it wouldn't work. I don't know why I keep doing this to myself. It is just stupid to keep trying."

The reason people keep seeking is the fact people really do want to simplify their life as long as they don't have to change anything to get it. Think about it – isn't that really humorous?

They want a better life while maintaining the same design! Why? I think they are fearful of getting out of the routine they have designed for their life, and what would happen if they break free of that design. It is much easier to make statements, to talk about what you intend on doing, than it is to break out of the routines you build you life upon.

Here is the interesting thing about Making Simple, Simple it is all based on one question you ask yourself. This question is about slowing your life down, learning to take a deep breath and looking at what your behavior will bring to your life.

Ready to learn that one question that will Simply Make Your Life Simple? Before you say "YES!" to anything, and I mean anything, pause, take a deep breath and ask yourself:

Is this decision going to feed my confusion or strengthen my clarity?

Does that sound difficult? It's just you understanding the direction your choice will take your life. It's you taking responsibility for your life. The answer to this one question will either bring confusion or clarity to your life. Look at the question! It presents you with two options – confusion or clarity. What other option is there for you to go?

When you feel comfortable and confident with your decision, you move in that direction. Clarity creates a pace you can manage, a belief this is right for you and the feeling that you can do it.

Now, many have asked me, "How do I really know if something is confusion or clarity?" Great question!

Here is the difference. Confusion always carries with it fear, doubt and uncertainty. Clarity always brings you a sense of calmness with your choice, an understanding of what is involved and your willingness to commit to the journey.

How many times have you made a decision while you were feeling confused, and in a short time realized it was the wrong decision? Have you been there, done that and bought the T-shirt?

As simple as this question is, what makes it so complex? The fact it's a question! When you ask a question, you must be willing to listen to the answer. The majority of questions people ask are really looking for the path to confusion.

How many times have you heard:
- I don't ask because I don't want the answer!
- I didn't ask for you to tell me.
- I won't ask because I'm okay with things the way they are.

Each of these are asked to keep sameness as the design for your life. My philosophy is simple – If you're not going to do anything, stop saying you are!

I guarantee you if you will take this Simple Truth, this little question and for the next 30 days use it as the focused guide book for your decision making and are willing to say "NO!" to anything that takes you toward confusion, you will find yourself on the other side with a much simpler life.

If you REALLY want a simpler life, you have to start somewhere and this is it – Is this going to feed my confusion or strengthen my clarity? Starting the journey toward the simple life is as easy as asking this simple question!

How Do You Make This Simple Question Your Foundation For Decision Making?

S STAY AT A PACE YOU CAN MANAGE

I INVEST IN BEING CLEAR ABOUT WHAT YOU WANT FOR YOUR LIFE

M MANAGE THE TERRAIN YOU ARE TRAVELING

P PAUSE WHEN YOU BEGIN TO FEEL OVERWHELMED

L LOOK FROM WHERE YOU ARE, NOT WHERE YOU'VE BEEN

E ENTER EACH DAY MENTALLY PREPARED

Chapter 3

You Can Really Make a Mess Out of Your Life!

Life can really be simple, until you bring behaviors to your life that take the simple out of simple.

Alice and John came to me and ask if I would help them get their life, their marriage back on track. They were high school sweethearts and married right out of high school. That was 15 years prior.

As John put it, "life was so much simpler then. We were just getting started and everything was new and filled with adventure and excitement. We didn't have a care in the world. We were in love and that was all that mattered."

He looked at Alice and then continued. "Three years later our first son, Peter, was born. We thought we were ready for children, but in hind sight, we should have waited a few more years."

At this point Alice jumped in. "We had told ourselves we would wait for at least five years so we could get established, get our feet under us, but there was this constant pressure from both our parents to give them a grandchild. We are both only children, and our parents kept pushing us to give them a grandchild. Looking back, we should have told them we weren't ready, but their pressure was relentless. So, we gave in. We were both still kids. Two years after Peter was born we had Megan. At that point we were ready to have another child. Neither of us wanted Peter to be an only child. We didn't want him to grow up the way we did."

"Richard," John said, "Don't get us wrong. We love our two children. They are a big part of our life. The struggle is having Peter before we were ready started a path of confusion we haven't been able to get off of. Oh, both our parents are happy. It's just we want to simplify our life. We are both tired of this rat race we are living. We both know having a child is a blessing, but if you have them before you are ready and they are an interruption, rather than a blessing, it's hard. It put so much financial pressure on us. We had a plan that included having children, but not as early as we did. Our life is now focused on the kids, not us and our family. We need to get back to being in control of our life, rather than our life controlling us."

Reaching over and grabbing each other's hand, they both ask at the same time. "Can you help us rediscover what it means to have a simple life?"

John looked at me and said, "We know it is possible, but we don't know how to get there!"

Art approached me as I was walking off the golf course, put his arm around my shoulder and said, "I hear you are the man who can fix any life!"

We both chuckled. I stopped, looked at him and said, "I can't fix broken, because I don't have any glue that strong."

He laughed, looked at me and with a deep concern on his face said, "Richard, I have really messed up my life, and I don't know what to do. I am drowning in my emotions and can't seem to get my head above water. My life use to be so simple, and then, I royally screwed it up. The sad thing was I knew what I was doing was the wrong thing to do, but my ego was so out of control. At that moment I just didn't care. I wanted what I wanted, and I wasn't going to listen to anyone. Man, what a mess I have made for myself."

Over the years I have met so many John's and Alice's, so many Art's! They are like so many. They give into the pressure that is dumped on them; they go against what they know is right for their life. They take a life that had purpose, a design and choose to mess it up.

You've been there! You were walking a path that was taking your life forward. You had a dream you were working to make happen. Then, out of the blue, you decided to take the simple and mess it up. Why? Why would you do that to yourself? Can I suggest there are four major reasons someone as smart, as intelligent, as you would choose to take the simple out of simple.

First, you **make decisions based solely on your emotions.** I believe you either live from your emotions up or your mind down. The challenge is, whichever one you choose sets the direction for your life and creates the pathway you walk.

When you choose to live from your emotions down you don't let your mind, your creative center, have a part in the decision making process. Your emotions are in control and that can create a major mess. When your emotions are leading the way, the decisions you make are mostly guided by "what if." With "what if" as the foundation for making the decision, you don't think! Take your mind out of the equation and you don't have a clear path to walk.

Second, you **explain things away and don't hold yourself accountable for your behavior.** Anytime you choose to explain your behavior away with excuses, blame or the fact the devil made you do it, you are going to mess your life up. In my book, Behavior Never Lies, I address what the lack of accountability brings to your life. The reality is your life is your life. Others are part of your life; they may have an affect on your life, but this is your life! You make the choices; you implement the behavior, and you live out your choices through your behavior. As long as you have an escape plan, you take the simple out of your life being simple.

Third, you **start to do what you know is right for you, and then, revert back to your old behavior because of fear.** Here is what I find interesting about human behavior—you know what is right and what is wrong for your life. It is not a mystery. You really do know! You start down the right path and then, come face to face with fear. That fear increases your emotions, fills you with doubt, and makes the path look like a jungle there is no way through. Now, what you knew was right, becomes what you feel is wrong. At that moment you are frozen in time. At that point you are confused and the confusion paralyzes you, and you make the right wrong and the wrong right.

Fourth, you **struggle with the opinions of others and give them control of your life.** How strong are you? Are you strong enough to resist those who want to control you life? Are you strong enough to say "NO" when "NO" is the right answer?

You must always remember that you don't lose control of your life; YOU choose to give it away. When YOU lack the trust, the belief, in yourself, YOU become a very weak person. YOU must have strength and trust in YOUR life to make YOUR life YOUR life; YOU must have the faith, the trust, the belief in yourself. YOU must make your life, YOUR life. When YOU live giving control of YOUR life to others, YOU have really messed up YOUR life.

Fact is, *most don't have that level of faith and trust in their self!* The majority of people don't trust their self, don't believe in their self, don't have the confidence to stand up to those who want to own them and program their life.

When you don't trust, believe or have confidence in you, you give your life away, and there is always someone who wants to program you with what they feel is right for your life. The reality is they don't care about YOU! They may say they do, but their agenda is not about you. It is about what they want to use you for or what they want to steal from you. Either way, they bring a selfish agenda, and you become a tool they use and then, throw away.

Your life becomes a mess when you are not strong enough to make it your life. There is no simple in becoming someone's hostage.

Do you understand when you don't like you, don't believe in you, don't trust yourself, you exist looking for someone you feel loves you, wants the best for you. Both of these are the farthest things from the truth. They really want to own you and make you their emotional slave.

Look at these four:

- You make decisions based solely on your emotions.
- You explain things away and don't hold yourself accountable for your behavior.
- You start to do things you know are right for your life, and then revert back to old behavior because of fear.
- You struggle with the opinions of others and give them control of your life.

Can you see how each of these creates a pathway of self-destruction? Can you see how each of these creates a life that can only end up as a mess?

If You Have Made a Mess Out of Your Life, How Do You Start Cleaning It Up?

S   START WITH HOLDING YOURSELF ACCOUNTABLE FOR THE CHOICES YOU HAVE MADE

I   INSIST ON SLOWING THE PACE OF YOUR LIFE DOWN

M   MANAGE EVERY DECISION WITH LIFE'S ONE QUESTION

P   PAUSE WHEN YOU KNOW YOU HAVE MADE A MESS, CLARIFY YOUR DECISION, RETHINK AND MOVE IN THE RIGHT DIRECTION

L   LISTEN TO WHAT YOUR MIND IS TELLING YOU

E   EXTRACT THE LESSONS YOU HAVE LEARNED AND LET GO OF THE REST

Chapter 4

Why Would You Choose to Mess Up Your Life?

You lose the Simple Life when you start making decisions that bring confusion to your life. It really is as simple as that!

So, do you spend more time in your life feeding your confusion or strengthening your clarity? Are most the decisions you make about your life thought out or do you make emotional decisions, implement and then, pause and think about what you have done?

The question about *feeding your confusion or strengthening your clarity* is paramount to having a simple life. You do one or the other. If you can think of another choice, let me know. I have found in life you are always doing one or the other.

This is your life! There is only so much of it, because there is an expiration date. The choices you make today create the tomorrow you will live. When you fully understand that, you will slow down, look at what you are choosing to do and make the choice that will take your life forward.

The challenge is:
Give me 10 people who are faced with a decision, and 8 of them will choose the pathway to confusion!

Why would any sane person knowingly choose to take their life away from having a simple life and choose to make their life difficult through the decision they make. Let's answer this by studying human behavior.

The first reason they would choose confusion over clarity is their **past and its wrongs are what they use to view their life.**

Charlotte is a perfect example. Her yesterday was not the best. She grew up with an abusive father and a mother who would never confront anything.

Her father was both emotionally and physically abusive. When he was drunk, he would beat her for no reason. She could never do anything right. He was always beating her emotionally by telling her how stupid she was, and he couldn't believe he has such a dumb child.

Her mother would never say anything. She would stay away from her, because if she tried to help Charlotte, he would turn on her. It was easier for her mother to avoid, than confront what he said.

Now, what do you think Charlotte grew up thinking about herself? What kind of men do you think she would bring to her life?

Her life was a mess! She was so desperate for someone to love, she would reach out to anyone who paid attention to her. This made her an easy target for anyone who could sense how desperate she was.

My challenge was getting her to face the design she had created for her life. Her past created her present. All she knew was what her father programmed her to feel about herself.

She would keep asking me, "How do I get rid of all this?"

My answer was always, "Charlotte, we can't erase yesterday, but we can redesign how you view yourself."

When you have had a self destructive yesterday, it takes a strong desire to not let it continue to be the design for your present. So many who have had that type of yesterday carry it with them everyday.

If you can't let go of the negatives of yesterday, you can't have a today that is better.

The second reason they would choose confusion over clarity is **expectation for their life are designed around a sense of low self-esteem**.

What you feel about yourself creates the reasons you make the decisions you make. If you don't love you, you will not see yourself as lovable! If you don't trust yourself, you will doubting every decision you make. If all you have known is confusion in your in your life, you will examine every experience from your emotions up. The result will be a continuing expectation that things are only going to get worse. Ed is a perfect example. He lived believing he had a perpetual dark cloud over his head. Things could be going great, and he would find something wrong. Then, look at you and say, "See I told you my life was cursed!"

He had no trust in himself! When it came to making a decision, he could know was the right thing to do, but choose the wrong path. His reasoning, *"Things in my life have never gone right, so why should I think it is going to be any different now. I am doomed to live a life of misery."*

Words cannot really emphasize the importance of believing in and trusting yourself. When these two are not the foundation for making the decisions for your life, you are going to choose confusion over clarity.

Ed told me one day, "I wouldn't know what to do if my life was simple. It is a waste of time and good air to believe it is going to be any better than it is now."

The third reason they would choose confusion over clarity is **resisting change is their way of looking at the future.**

Do you think change is frightening for most people? Just look at yourself – how much stress do you bring to your life because you fight what you know is right, but to accept it means you have to CHANGE!

When there is a pathway to improving your life, and you resist because it means *you are going to have to change your behavior*, you lock yourself in the Circle of Sameness. Oh, you talk about what you plan on doing, what you intend to become, the changes you are going to make, but when you walk to the front door of decision, you look at what you are going to do and make tomorrow when you will do it.

Learn this, *most people resist change because of the fear they have attached to it.* When change and fear join forces, the result is resistance.

Can you see how this plays into why most people choose confusion over clarity? When your past is your present, which has created a sense of low self-esteem and to improve you are going to have bring change into your life, think there won't be resistance to what you know you should do? The result is you fighting the path to clarity and choosing confusion.

This was Anthony. His words to me were, "Everyone tells me you are the man who can help me with my life. They say you won't force me to do anything, but will challenge me with questions. Here is my problem! I want a better life, but if it means changing my life, I am afraid I can't do that. The most frightening word in my life is 'Change.' I know it is the right thing, but my fear of the unknown is so great, I run any time I have to come face to face with the reality of what I must do."

The simple truth is *you can't improve until you accept Change as the starting point.* If you can't, you will continue to feed your confusion, rather than strengthen your clarity.

The fourth reason they would choose confusion over clarity is a **sense of purpose is missing from their life.**

Purpose is the reason you do what you do! When you can't define your purpose, you are going to live with confusion as your stumbling block.

Walter put it this way. "Richard, I get up every day lost. I get up, get ready and go to a job I don't like, but it gives me a pay check."

There was this long pause before he continued. "If I were

honest with you, I really don't feel like I have a life. I just exist from day to day, and I have been this way for years. I am so tired of living this way. The disappointment, the frustration, the lack of living is just emotionally taking over my life. I have got to find a purpose for my life. I have got to find the reason I am on this earth! I don't want to get up each day feeling this way!"

I wish I could say Walter is the exception, rather than the rule. The simple truth is there are a million Walter's out there. They get up each day trapped in a world where they exist – *they don't live!* When many start feeling this way, they work hard to find a way out of the misery they get up each day facing. Because they seek to do it their self, they sink deeper into their world of feeling lost. Their lack of joy, happiness, fulfillment and desire to know why they are on this earth becomes the life they accept. The result is they accept their trapped life and slip into an acceptable form of depression. They find moments of joy, but can't sustain them. The highs and lows of their life keep them in a confusion, which they accept as their life. They feel this is simply the way their life was meant to be. Their purpose becomes keeping their life as it is, where it is and not stressing their self out over what they feel they will never be able to achieve.

The fifth reason they would choose confusion over clarity is **others have control of the direction of their life.**

Throughout the chapter of this book I have continually challenged you to understand *this is your life! It is yours to design, to control, to create, to live!* In my years of working with human behavior I have found this to be a common struggle. When you live in confusion, it becomes difficult to see anything except the confusion you are living in. You don't want to be here, but you don't know what to do to get out of this emotional jungle. So, someone looks at you and says, "Here is what you need to do." Because you want out so badly, you move toward them, hear what they are saying, and follow their design for your life.

Here is the sad part to this – *when you do that, it is no longer your life.* In that you give up your individuality. You lose YOU! You are their captive; you emotionally belong to them.

You have no idea how many times I am asked, "Are you a motivational speaker?" My answer is always "NO!" The look on faces is priceless.

Dan asked me that question and when I gave him my answer, the look on his face was one of surprise. "I am here for you to motivate me! That is why I came."

"Well, you are in the wrong place. Dan, I can't motivate anyone. Motivation is a personal drive. If I motivated you, I would have to adopt you, God knows I don't want to do that!"

I paused to let him absorb what I was saying and calm the feelings that were being expressed on his face.

"Dan, motivation is a set of emotions that are attached to your desire for your life. If you don't have a dream, a purpose, that 'something' you really want for your life and are willing to pay the price to obtain, you will lack the personal motivation necessary to push your life forward. Does that make sense to you?"

"I think so. What you are saying is 'I am responsible for me.' What if I don't like that idea? I have grown up with everyone telling me who I am, what I should be doing. As long as I am doing what they want me to do, they like me. BUT, when I disagree with them or no longer want to do what they tell me I should be doing, they go away. That has been my life.

I have never had to be responsible for me!"

"Dan, that's the reason your life is the way it is. You are not an individual. You are what the flavor of the month is for your life. Would you say you live in confusion?"

"Confusion!" He laughed out loud and continued, "I think I am way beyond being confused. I am not even sure I am alive. If I don't have someone telling me what to do, I feel dead."

Each day, in so many different ways, the Dan's of life stumble through their life. They don't seem to understand *when it is no longer your life, you don't have a life – just an existence.*

Hear me and hear me with an open mind!! *Anyone who wants to have control of your life wants to use you for their selfish agenda.* As long as you live by their agenda, they love you and use you. When they get tired of playing with your life, or you get tired of feeling used, they throw you away. Emotionally, they dump you into pit where you now don't know what to do. The confusion you feel is a form of depression that results from you no longer have any ideas what to do. For many, they go searching for someone else to take care of them – to give their life to. This vicious circle becomes a way of life for them.

The sixth reason they would choose confusion over clarity is **no longer are they willing to work to free their self from the confusion that owns their life. They have given up!**

People do give up! That is so a tragic fact. They reach a point where their internal message is, *"Why try! Nothing is going to be any different than what my life is right now."*

Giving up is the result of the five things we have been discussing here. When "what is" is all you can "see" for your life, giving up becomes the chosen option.

When you give up, you stop searching; you stop believing; you live from yesterday to today; you are convinced that this is "all there is to life."

When I think of a life that has given up, Joy comes to my mind. I met her while I was the Baptist Campus Minister at Ohio University. It was common for the University to send people to me for counseling.

I was in my office when there was a knock at my door. "Come in!"

The door opened and as I looked up I saw what I can only describe as a *shadow of life.* Have you ever meet someone whom you felt was a presence without life? That was Joy.

"Come in, come in. Hi, I'm Richard."

"I know who you are. My counselor said I needed to talk to you."

"What's your name?"

"I'm Joy, but my name is a lie about me. I have no Joy. I don't know why they sent me to see you. I really don't have anything to say to you or talk about. I guess I am here, because they said you were good at helping people fix their life. Are you?"

"Well, I can't fix a life, but I can help those who want a better life find the way forward. Is that what you are looking for?"

"You have to have a life to be able to fix it, right?"

"Joy, everyone has a life, but not everyone knows how to live their life. It sounds like you have lost your purpose for your life."

"Lost it! I don't think I have ever had it. If you know me, you would understand why I say that. I have given up on ever having a life. I just wish I had something that would make me feel like I have a reason for being on this earth."

"Hey, you woke up this morning. You have been given another day living. Isn't that something to be thankful for?"

"I get up most mornings wishing I was dead. I don't want to get out of bed; I don't want to face people; I don't want to do anything."

She paused, took a very deep breath and said with tears starting to run down her face, "I can't find a reason to live. I don't want to die, but I don't want to live. Doesn't that make me crazy?"

"NO! It doesn't make you crazy. It says you are trapped in a world where you can't see options. You only see what you are feeling in the moment. You can't see a pathway out of where you are. Joy, that is being trapped in your own life of being lost. Until you can find that path, and it does exist, you are going to sink deeper and deeper into an existence without meaning. We can find that path!!"

"I have felt this way for years. I have given up on ever finding anything different than what I have right now. I use to try, but each time I took one step forward I got knocked three steps back. You can only take that so long, and you soon tell yourself, 'what's the use.' That is what I feel right now about my life."

Giving up on life is real for many people. When you reach the point of "giving up on your life," you are trapped in an emotional jungle where everywhere you look there is just more jungle to have to deal with. When you can't see a pathway forward, no matter how hard you try, you live without a positive thread to hang onto. You live in a constant state of confusion.

I will say it to you again, ***there is no simple in confusion!*** Confusion is a thief that steals the simple from your life. As long as you exist in confusion, you will continue to mess up your life. The bigger the mess you create for yourself, the further you move from *living a simple life.*

By the way, if you could meet Joy today, she owns her own business, married with two children and enjoying the path her life is on.

How Can You Know When You Are Living In Confusion?

L   LOOK AT THE DIRECTION OF YOUR LIFE – CIRCLES OR FORWARD

I   INTERNALLY YOU ARE STRUGGLING WITH BEING MOTIVATED

V   VICTORIES ARE FAR AND FEW BETWEEN

I   INVESTING IN YOURSELF SEEMS POINTLESS

N   NO SENSE OF DIRECTION FOR YOUR LIFE

G   GIVING UP ON HAVING A BETTER LIFE IS A STRONG OPTION

Chapter 5

6 Steps to Making Your Life Simply, Simple

There is always a process to take you to simple.

The big question – *do you think a life can create a simple lifestyle?* I do, but not without a plan, not without a commitment to make the necessary changes and not without being willing to take an internal look through the eyes of personal honesty.

Now, do you think that would make the journey to *making your life simply simple challenging?* You know the answer is YES! Anything that takes you out of your uncomfortable, comfortable routine is going to take a lot of focused energy.

Here is one thing I know for a fact – *most people want to simplify their life! They just don't know how to achieve it.* I can't begin to tell you the number of conversations I have had with people where the conversation has turned to one statement – *what we are seeking to do is simplify our life.* It is a constant conversation with people. I have found many are tired of the rat race they have created for their self. It seems the simple has become a foreign concept tied to some mysterious formula. The harder they try the more complex their life becomes.

Rhonda and Gil put it this way. "We have lived this treadmill lifestyle so long we have become addicted to it. There is never a week that goes by we don't talk about getting out of this style of living. The challenge is all we do is talk about it. We really do want out, but we can't figure out how to do it."

Peter put it this way. "I am only 28, but I feel I have no life. Yes, I am a perfectionist; yes, I push myself; yes, I promised myself I wouldn't get trapped in the same trap I watched my parents live for all my life. What I am watching myself do is put more and more stress on myself under the notion I am working to simplify my life. I will tell you I am a bigger mess now more than I have ever been. I've got to do something about this!"

Jeff and Sarah said this to me. "What is wrong with us? We

use to have such a simple life, and we were proud of that fact. We have to tell you that is no longer true about us. It is like we have fallen off the cliff and can't seem to find the trail back up. We have gotten to the place where we are never satisfied with what we have. There seems to always be something more, and we have to have it. It is insane, but it has become a compulsion with us. We work to break free, but the more we work to get back to normal (whatever that is) the more confusing life becomes. "

On and on I could go with stories people keep talking to me about. Yes, having a simpler life is a quest many people are searching for, but in the process the more stress they find their self struggling with. Can you identify with any of this? Do you ever look at your life and tell yourself, "Life can't be this difficult!" Do you ever say to yourself, "How did I (we) get our self in this mess?"

One gentleman said to me recently on a flight. "It seems like I took a wrong turn with the decisions I made with my life and now there is no way to reverse what I have done. Man, I just want my life back!"

Does your life have to be a mess? NO! Can a life be simplified? YES! Is there some way to get to a simple life? The answer is YES!

If you are searching for a simpler life, I can offer you a 6 Step Plan to **Making Your Life Simply Simple**. Are these steps magical? NO! Are they going to demand being willing to make changes to the way your life is right now? YES!

I will tell you they are mentally and emotionally challenging, but if you will take them one step at a time, not get in a hurry to achieving them and give your self permission to make the necessary improvement, these 6 Steps will allow you to **Make Your Life Simply Simple.**

Making Your Life Simply Simple

Chapter 6

Step 1: Start With Facing Where Your Life Is Right Now!

Where is your life right now? Is it in yesterday, tomorrow or today? Yes, each has its purpose, but the real lesson in simplify your life is in understanding how this triad works together to strengthen your life.

Yesterday is about *where you have been.* The conclusion of each Today creates a Yesterday. That Yesterday is important as a reference library. From Yesterday you take experiences; those experiences are placed in your new Today. Most of your understandings about what is happening in Today are defined by what you have taken from yesterday. It makes Yesterday a valuable part of how you are defining your life. If you take the negatives, you create a negative today. If you take the positives, the lessons, you strengthen your journey forward.

Today can be a repeat of Yesterday or it can be an opportunity to work on your new adventure. The challenge is too many bring their pain, their worries, their doubts of Yesterday into Today and create a continuation of the stress Yesterday had in their life. The result is the lack of a better space in their life. If Today is all about continuing Yesterday's turmoil, it will not be about growth. The more you relive Yesterday, the more confusion you bring to your life. The constant repeating of Yesterday leaves your mind wondering *when are we going to get through this.*

Tomorrow is what is in front of you, not where you are standing. When all your anticipation is about what you are going to do Tomorrow, you will waste the "Now" you have.

We teach so much about planning and granted we all need a plan, BUT that plan must be about Today, not Tomorrow. Tomorrow is an illusion; it is not reality, because it is not here yet. Yes Tomorrow is important, but if I by-pass Today, I will create confusion about Tomorrow before it even gets here.

Step 1: Start With Facing Where Your Life Is Right Now!

You cannot live in Tomorrow. You can prepare for it, but since it isn't real, you cannot live there. The only space you have for living is NOW! When you are projecting tomorrow, and that is all you are looking at, you are creating confusion for your life. You leave your mind wondering *how are we going to achieve this*. Preparation starts with taking the lessons from Yesterday and implementing them into Today through the correct behavior. When Tomorrow arrives and becomes the New Today, you are not the same person you were Yesterday.

Today is all you have. It is your NOW! What you do with your NOW, creates what you are preparing for in your life.

It's really *simple* to understand. Yesterday is your past; Tomorrow is your future; Today is your NOW. Today is the only time and space you have. Today is the bridge that connects Yesterday to Tomorrow. The strength of Today is all about the lessons you have implemented from Yesterday. The Power of Tomorrow is being created by what you are doing with your NOW – your Today.

Wally met me for breakfast. He had called in a panic saying, "Richard, you have to see me. You just have to!"

I agreed, and as he entered the restaurant I could feel his energy before he got to the table. Everything about his presence was a statement of a life out of control.

"Wally, you are a mess! I could feel your presence before you got to the table."

"You got that right. I have been a mess for a long time, but now I am even a bigger mess."

"What's going on?"

"I'm lost and I mean REALLY lost. I have no dream, no energy, no purpose and I guess with all of that no life."

"Are you alive?"

"Barely! Richard, I can't shake the pain I have been through. When Joyce left, my life ended. All I do is sit around and think about Yesterday. I replay so many old tapes. I beat on myself for all the dumb things I did. Each day is just a repeat of what I went through Yesterday, and it is killing me. I have to stop living this way, but I don't know how!"

"Wally, what have you learned from all you have been through?"

"Other than the fact that I am a dumb idiot?"

"What have you learned that can make your life different? You know all the things you did wrong, so what do you need to do differently with your life so you don't repeat those behaviors?"

There was a pause and eyes that were blank. "Richard, I don't know. All I can think about is what I did wrong."

"Wally, that's your issue. You are not *learning from* where you have been. You are simply *dragging it along with you.* In doing that you can't get through it. You have to find a quiet place where you can take a deep breath and change your sight plan. You have to learn from what you did wrong. The truth is you can't go back and undo what you have done. What you can do is look at the behaviors that created the situation, understand why you did those things and create a plan of commitment to not repeat them. This means you have to implement the lessons into each New Today, so you can become a New Wally, rather than a continuation of the Old Wally. Until you can do that, you will continue to drag, not learn."

I'll bet you know a Wally. I would bet you know someone who spends their time *dragging* Yesterday through Today. The result of this behavior is not being able to stand in their NOW. *To Simplify your life You Must Stand In Your Now! You must face your life from where you are right now.*

Step 1: Start With Facing Where Your Life Is Right Now!

Will that always be easy? NO! But it has to be the starting point. It is about learning the power of "Beginning Anew." You take the Yesterday you had, extract the lessons you learned and implement them into Today. Until you can do that, you will drag the pain, the messes, of yesterday into Today. Now which one will feed your confusion and which one will strengthen your clarity?

Simple Keys To Facing Your "Now"

K Keep your life at a manageable pace

E Entertain new ideas that challenge your thinking

Y You must be moving from today to tomorrow

S Stay in the present

Chapter 7

Step 2: Invest Your Time In Cleaning Up The Clutter In Your Life!

Do you live with any stacks in your life? I mean piles you have created and look at through the eyes of good intention. You know the stacks are there; you keep having conversations with yourself and with others about cleaning them up, BUT those stacks just keep slipping off your radar.

Those stacks are Clutter! Those stacks are emotional thieves! Those stacks are mental roadblocks. Hear me, your mind cannot see beyond Clutter. The fact they are there, the fact you keep telling yourself you are going to do something about them, the fact you never get to them shuts your mind down. Your mind seeks clarity; Clutter creates confusion! Get the picture!!

Can you see how this would create a war between your mind and your emotions? Your mind wants things to be simple, and Clutter makes that impossible. Your emotions give you permission to procrastinate, and procrastination gives you permission to waste the most precious gift you have – time. When Clutter and procrastination join forces, you create a mess that keeps you walking around the things you need to complete. Anything you start, but don't complete creates Clutter, Confusion and a Mess for you to stare at.

I finished my seminar on "Achieving Organization," was putting my computer away and here came Alice. She walked to the front row, fell in the chair, stared at me for a moment and said, "You are a curse and a blessing! I saw the title of your program in the Conference Guide and thought, 'I need to go hear this,' but at the same time said to myself, 'Oh, you know what you need to do why waste your time there.' It was another of those inner battles I go through."

She paused, smiled and was waiting for me to say something. I turned a chair around, looked at her and just

Step 2: Invest Your Time In Cleaning Up The Clutter In Your Life!

remained silent."

"You're waiting on me, aren't you?"

I nodded "Yes," and that was all she needed to go on with her story.

"I am the collector of Clutter you were talking about. When you talked about a desk so stacked with stuff, you can't see the top of it. When you mentioned the trunk of your car being a collection center, that was me. When you talked about your garage so packed with things, you can't get your car in, that is my life."

I smiled and she laughed. "You are enjoying this aren't you? You nailed me, and it made me very uncomfortable. Richard, I keep telling myself I have to do something about this. It is not only driving me crazy, but my husband and kids. If you walked into my office, you wouldn't be able to find a place to sit. If you looked in our formal dining room, the table is covered with 'stuff' I need to get to. I don't think I am a hoarder. I think I am just a messed up person who is so busy being busy I have gotten my life out of control. I haven't always been this way. I used to be the most organized person you could meet, BUT somewhere along the way that woman went on vacation and hasn't come back. My husband keeps asking 'What happened to that over organized woman I married,' and I tell him I don't know where she went. I need to get her back. Thank You for your information today. I think you may have awakened my inner spirit to do something, rather than talk about what I am going to do."

"Give me your phone number. I am going to call you in a week to see whether this has just been more chatter or if you are serious about taking control of your life. Clutter is a thief and a feeder of your confusion."

A week later I called her, and she asked if she could have an email address where she could send me some pictures. When I got them, they were before and after pictures of her office. I was amazed at how much she had achieved.

I called her and told her how proud I was of her. This was her response to me, "Richard, first Thank You for taking the time to talk to me. I love the fact you listened and didn't condemn. I have to tell you *my life is so much simpler without this clutter.* My husband and kids took me out to dinner and told me they were proud of what I had done. But, I am not done yet. I am like this mad woman now wanting to get all this cleared up."

Stacks steal the simple out of life! Where there is a stack that needs attention, there is confusion. Where there is confusion, there can't be Simple!

Simple Keys For Cleaning Up Clutter

K KEEP COMMITTED TO COMPLETING WHAT YOU START

E EXECUTE A PLAN OF PERSONAL ORGANIZATION

Y YOU MUST SEE CLUTTER AS AN ENEMY AND A THIEF

S STACKS BECOME A NO, NO

Chapter 8

Step 3: Make Time For Yourself!

Serious question: *Where do you fit into your own life?* Do you live to take care of everyone else or do you allow yourself to be a priority in your own life? Yes, there is a need to apply both to your life. When you do, you create balance in your life. Do you have that word "Balance" as a part of your life? Where Balance is missing, confusion is present.

Most people struggle with having Balance in their life. They live with one or the other – they either spend their time taking care of everyone around them, or they lose their self in doing what they want to do without any concern for the others in their life.

Balance is an aspect of life that is challenging to achieve. Most of the lack of balance in your life is the result of you not knowing how to prioritize your life. So many times this is the result of trying to juggle too many things. How many times have you had more to do than you could manage? How many days do you get up and look mission impossible right in the face?

Balance is about learning to say NO! Have you ever said NO, but did it anyway? "NO!" is a word of control. To make it an okay word for your life, you must take guilt out of the picture. As long as you live feeling guilty about what you aren't doing, what you didn't do, you are going to wrestle with confusion and deny your life Simple!

Making Your Life Simply Simple is about taking control of your life. Now, some would say I am promoting you becoming totally selfish. I'm not! You were not put on this earth to be the caretaker of everyone in your life. If you do that, you have no life. Yes, you are to help. Yes, you are to give others part of your time, BUT not sacrifice your life to take care of them.

Step 3: Make Time For Yourself!

Many are going to disagree with me here, BUT your value to others begins with your value to yourself. How many times have you been angry, because there was no time left for you? How many times have you been frustrated, because everyone came to you to take care of what they could do? How many times have you wanted to run away and hide where no one could find you?

The Key is to find a sense of Balance in your life. I hope you have lived long enough to realize most people are not going to come to you and say, "Hey, why don't you take some time for yourself." It is your life, and you have to create Balance for yourself. It is not selfish to want time for you. It is not wrong to tell people NO! It is not wrong to make yourself a priority in your own life. You must teach others that *your value to them begins with you having time for you.* When you are frustrated, how much confusion can you bring to yourself and others? When you have Balance, how much simpler does your life become? Get over the idea *you are here to serve others and forget about what you want for your life.*

I was in a marriage counseling session with Maureen and Justin. I knew them from the couples class in the church. They were a fun couple on the outside, but when I watched them, I knew there were rough waters under what appeared to be a quiet ocean. Finally, one day they sought me out after church and asked, "Would you have some time to talk to us?"

I inwardly smiled, and we set an appointment. When they arrived, I had set the room with three chairs positioned so they would have to look at each other. They looked at the positioning of the chairs, looked at me and just stood there.

"Alright, stop staring at the chairs and sit down."

I pointed to where I wanted each of them to sit. "Okay

you two, what is going on?"

Justin looked at Maureen, and Maureen looked at Justin. I smiled and said, "We can sit here and you two stare at each other, or we can talk and understand what is going on. Your choice."

With that they both turned to me, and Maureen began. "Richard, we have been married for almost eight years, and I don't feel he appreciates me anymore."

With that Justin jumped in. "You know that is not true, and I don't understand why you feel that way. You know I love you more today than I did when we got married. Why are you saying that?"

I felt I needed to interject here. "Okay, we are not here to fight. We are here to find out what is going on and find a point of agreement, right?"

They both looked at me, and each nodded in agreement.

"Maureen, you started this conversation, so why don't you share with me why you don't feel Justin appreciates you."

She took a deep breath to keep the tears from coming and said in a very shaky voice, "Everything seems to be all about him. I feel like I have no voice in this relationship. If we plan something, it has to be what he wants to do. If I try to express an opinion, he either disagrees or just turns and walks away. If I want some time for ME, he makes me feel guilty for wanting some 'ME' time. I don't feel like I am a partner in this relationship. I feel like I am his personal slave."

"Justin, how do you feel about what she is saying?"

He started with a gruffness in his voice, which had a tone of anger in it.

"Justin, listen to yourself. You are gearing up for a war. This is not about who is right and who is wrong. It is about understanding what each is feeling. Until you two can sense the emotions here and understand why they are present, there will be no resolution. There will be only an increase in your confusion. Does that make sense?"

He paused, looked at me and then Maureen. "I'm sorry. It is just the fact we have been struggling with this for such a long time."

"Hey, what was your relationship like in the beginning?"

Justin looked at Maureen and continued. "It was so simple. We didn't argue or fight. We didn't have a problem making a decision. We talked, decided what we wanted and did it. It was a lot easier then."

"He is right. When we first started dating, we talked. He listened to me. I felt he was interested in what I had to say and appreciated my input. I feel that somewhere along the way we lost that connection."

"So Justin, let's go back to what Maureen was saying about not feeling appreciated. Do you understand where that is coming from?"

Justin looked down, paused for a few moment, looked at Maureen and said, "I really don't understand where this is coming from. We have a good life."

At that point, Maureen inserted, "As long as things go your way!"

"Hey you two. Remember we are not here to fight, but to find a resolution to what is happening. Go ahead Justin."

"Richard, I work real hard to give us a good life. My job is not easy and requires a lot of energy. I am tired when I finish a day, and just want to come home and relax. Maureen doesn't seem to understand that. There is always something she wants me to help her with. There is a discussion she wants to have, and I just want to rest. Is that wrong? On Saturdays I like to play golf with my friends, and she gets upset. I need that time to unwind. I don't get why she gets so upset over that."

"Richard," Maureen said. "It is not that I mind him doing things for himself. I know he works hard, and his job is not easy, but I have a busy life also. Here's the problem. When I want to do something for myself or my girlfriends, he gets upset. If I go anywhere, I get the third degree. He wants to know where I am going, when I am going to be back. It's like I live under his thumb. I need time for myself, just like he does, BUT that doesn't seem to matter to him."

"You two have lost the friendship connection between the two of you. You both seem to resent what the other one feels they need. You are like two children fighting for attention and not getting it. You each 'want' for yourself and not for each other. There has to be time for each of you to have personal time, but there also needs to be time for each other. You have no balance in your life. You look at each other through the eyes of 'what you feel is missing,' rather than the desire to 'help bring balance to each other.' Does that make sense?"

This is one of the greatest challenge in our fast paced, misuse of time and over stressed life style that has been created. The person who gets left in the dust is self. When life cannot be managed through making sure there is time for self, there is going to be confusion that feeds your anger, your disappointment, your frustrations. When these three join forces, there is no Simple in your life.

Step 3: Make Time For Yourself!

Simple Keys To Making Time For Yourself

K Keep "NO" as an option

E Exclude people who want to steal time from your life

Y Yearning for "me" time becomes a reality

S Sense how precious time is

Chapter 9

Step 4: Pause When You Feel Your Life Is Becoming Overwhelmed!

Do you ever feel your life is moving too fast? How many times have you felt there was too much to do and not enough time to get it all done?

I find it interesting how today there is this overwhelming feeling that you have to fill each day with as much as possible, YET when you look at your "To Do List," you know it's a mission impossible. But you choose to go forward knowing you are going to be frustrated and angry with what you don't get done. Have you ever been there?

So many talk to me about "all the pressure" society puts on them. The truth is "society doesn't put pressure on you." You do that to yourself. You can get so busy, being busy, doing busy stuff, there is no time for you to breathe. You come up for air only to discover there is still a lot of "stuff" waiting for you to do. Do you then pause and create a plan to take control? Most don't! They take a deep breath and jump back in only to create a bigger overwhelming mess to deal with.

Do you think this design can bring overwhelming confusion to your life?

You understand in this design *there is no time to rest, no time to catch your breath, no time to have that time for yourself!*

There is only more confusion to feed your emotions. Your enemy is not all the "stuff" there is for you to do. The enemy you are facing is YOU! You create a world you can't manage, and in that world the "stuff" manages YOU – YOU can't manage yourself!

From what I am seeing, this is not getting better; it is actually getting worse. This is not life's fault. It is you not willing to slow down and take control of the pace of your life. If you can't slow down and manage your life, your life will

Step 4: Pause When You Feel Your Life Is Becoming Overwhelmed!

continue to speed up and wear you out!

Remember, in an earlier chapter we talked about the fact *this is your life to design, to live, to find purpose and fulfillment in.* When you can't slow yourself down you overwhelm yourself with behaviors that are designed to put you on a self-destructive course with yourself. There is no Simple in that design – only more confusion for you to deal with.

I look at all the unhappy people there are, all those who live with their own form of depression, who can't seem to live without some form of medication. They find it easier to pop a pill, than face what their unresolved confusion is doing to their life.

I look at them and want to shout, "Life doesn't have to be this difficult! Slow down, don't make this a race, slow down and learn to enjoy the life you have. Time has an expiration date on it and you don't know when that is."

I find it interesting that many are on this treadmill life running faster and faster. Ask them why they are running so fast and most don't know what they are running to. They are just running, because that is what everyone else is doing. It has become like a flock of sheep running to the slaughter. Hear me – you can only run at an out of control pace for so long and then, it destroys the meaning of your life. The faster you run, the more confusion you create for yourself.

If you really want to **Make Your Life Simply Simple** you have got to know when and how to slow down. Simple comes when you know your purpose, your direction, have an agenda that keeps you stepping forward, have a strong commitment to get there and all this is build around a pace you can manage.

Bill is one of the greatest illustrations I know. He was a

friend, and we had several conversations about the pace of his life. He was on this treadmill lifestyle and seemed to just keep pushing the pace to another level.

One day I asked him, "Bill, what are you doing? Man, you can't keep this pace up without it doing physical damage to you."

"I know! Karen keeps telling me the same thing, but Richard, I am not getting any younger. I have made so many mistakes that have cost me the success I was working to achieve. I can't slow down. I feel I am so close to getting there."

"Bill, where is there?"

"You know! At that place in life where you feel successful."

"Stop! Look around your life. You have a great life. You and Karen are happy. The kids are gone, and you have the time now to do so much of what have talked about doing when the kids are gone."

"I know, but I just don't feel I am where I need to be. I am going to slow down. I know I just need a little more time, and I will be able to look in the mirror and tell myself 'I've made it!'"

It was a Thursday evening when I got the call from Karen. "Richard, I am at the hospital. Bill has had a heart attack."

"Is he okay?"

"I don't know. The doctors haven't told me anything yet. Can you come. He has been asking for you."

"I'll be there as quickly as I can."

When I arrived at the hospital, I found Karen with their two children sitting in the corner holding each other's hands.

Step 4: Pause When You Feel Your Life Is Becoming Overwhelmed!

"Have they told you anything yet?"

"NO! The nurse said the doctor should be out any minute."

Just as she spoke those words, the door open and the doctor made his way to Karen.

"How is he?"

"He is one lucky man. The heart attack was serious, but he got here soon enough we were able to minimize the damage. He is going to have to take it easy. He is not out of the woods yet."

The Doctor walked over to Karen, looked her squarely in the eyes and continued. "Karen, I told Bill several months ago he was on a collision course with himself. All the signs were there for this to happen. I warned him, and he promised me he would slow down and do a better job of taking care of himself. He is really lucky he is still alive."

Several days later I was in his hospital room. He looked at me when I entered the room and said, "I hope you are not another one here to tell me 'I told you so!' I don't need that."

He paused, turned to the window and continued. "The doctor told me I am one lucky person. Richard, my life was moving so fast, I didn't have time to listen to anyone. I just had to keep pushing myself. I guess I figured this would never happen to me. I've learned my lesson. What good is all this stuff I was chasing. I just wanted to prove I was better than the mistakes I had made in the past. Man, am I one dumb man."

"Bill, you are not dumb. You just seemed to have to prove yourself, when there was nothing to prove."

Do you think there are many Bill's in life? I do! They come in all sizes, all genders, all walks of life. They push and push and for the most part can't really tell you what they are pushing for. They get caught up in this treadmill lifestyle and can't turn it off. They know it is not healthy; they know it can kill them, but they just have to "have it all!"

You have to treat yourself with respect. You have got to manage your life and its pace, and not get caught up on the treadmill. You know when you are over stressed and overwhelmed and must pause and regroup. If you can't, it will kill you in many different ways.

Simple Keys To Keeping Your Life From Becoming Overwhelming

K KEEN SENSE OF YOUR EMOTIONAL LEVEL

E ENHANCE YOUR LEARNING ABOUT YOU

Y YOU TAKE CONTROL OF YOUR LIFE

S STAY AT A MANAGEABLE PACE

Chapter 10

Step 5: Let Go of The Wrongs of Yesterday

The direction of you life only goes in one of two directions –*you can go forward or go in circles.* If you can come up with any other life's direction, please let me know. As I have studied human behavior, I have found it is easier for most to live going in circles. They choose a repetitive life, rather than stepping outside their Circle of Sameness and take their life forward.

For many they feel Yesterday is a safe zone. It is what they know, and to think about challenging their self to go forward has too many fears to it. As I have worked with individuals, I have found there are two basic things they want. Now, they talk about all the things they want and are going to achieve, BUT when it comes down to their actual behavior, there are two basic desires that define their being – *feeling safe and feeling secure.*

Over and over as I have opened a life to their behavioral design, I have found these two to be the foundation for their decision making. Think about these two!

How important is feeling safe to you? Now, put that in context of either taking your life forward or staying in the Circle of Sameness you have created for yourself. Which do you think offer you the safest place to stay? When you life is not being challenged, you will live in confusion. The human spirit was designed for adventure, not hiding in Yesterday.

How important is security to you? What if taking my life forward interrupted my feeling of being secure? I can take my life forward and have to face the unknown, OR I can stay where I am feeling safe and that creates the feeling of security. Which do you think most would choose?

Truth is *there is really no safety or security in emotionally staying where you are living, only withering away.*

Step 5: Let Go of The Wrongs of Yesterday

You either make the choice to live from Yesterday to Today OR Today to Tomorrow! Look at your life – go on take this as a challenge. Look at your life! Which do you think is the prevalent design you are living?

When you MAKE the choice to live from Yesterday to Today, you are trapped in your fear. Now, again you need to hear me! Most of your fears are attached to something that went wrong in your yesterday. Wrongs paralyze us when the wrong is all we see and not the lesson. There is a lesson in every wrong. The challenge is *if all I am staring at is the pain the wrong created, I will hang onto it as a "reason I can't."*

Open your eyes, look around you, listen to what people say about moving their life forward and how many don't because of a wrong, an injustice they feel has been done to them.

I would bet there has been a time in your life when fear grabbed you and opened a door in your yesterday that was justified by a "wrong" you felt was done to you. Do you ever use it as an excuse, a justification, a reason why you can't go forward? Be honest with yourself. Do you think using that experience feeds your confusion or strengthens your clarity? Look at your life! Could you be doing more than you are doing right now, IF you could just let go of a wrong, an injustice, that you feel was done to you?

You are either a hostage to your yesterday, OR a pioneer to your future. Yes, wrongs are going to happen, pain is going to be created, scares are going to be there, BUT you don't have to let those things control your life. Your desire to go forward, to live from Today to Tomorrow, has got to be stronger than allowing yourself to exist with living from Tomorrow to Today.

Emotional pain is the result of a wrong being the only thing you feel. Every time your emotions take you back there, you grab for the pain and use it as a reason, an excuse, a point of blame or a justification for what you are not doing with your life right now.

There is a lesson to learn in every wrong. To find the lesson you have to take your emotional eye off the "wrong" and place it on what you have or can learn from this experience. Living a life of "wrongs," strengthen your confusion. It won't let you move beyond it. Too many times you are not looking for the lesson. YOU are looking for the point of blame, and that makes you a hostage to that experience.

To make your life simply simple, YOU have to let go of the wrongs of Yesterday. As long as the "wrongs" are your living room, you will be trapped in living from Yesterday to Today.

This was the greatest behavioral change I had to make in my life. If you know my life story (if not you need to read my book <u>Breaking Free</u>), you know when I was 16 my adopted parents gave me a suitcase, and I was left to find my way through life.

You want to talk about fear! Trying standing on a street corner at the age of 16 with nothing but a suitcase. Stand in the middle of a street and watch your adopted dad drive off after telling you, *don't you ever forget, I love you very much.*

Think about all the emotions that were racing through me.

"What did I do that was so bad, they didn't want me."

"My real mother didn't want me, and now my adopted parents don't want me either. I must be a terrible person."

Think about sitting on a window ledge seven stories

up in a hotel and wrestling with whether you should jump. I remember the emotional feeling that was saying to me, "Hey, there is nothing for you to live for. You might as well just stop all this pain."

Think this hasn't played with me? Think I haven't struggled overcoming what my adopted mother would tell me almost every day of my life?

You are the stupidest child I have ever known!
You will never amount to anything in your life!
I am sorry we ever adopted you. I didn't want you and will be glad when I don't have to look at you!

Do you think those three statements created pain for me? Do you think I had a rough time facing and working through them? Yes, for years I allowed them to define whom I was. BUT, that day I went back to face my adopted mom and dad, because I knew if I didn't, I would never get past these emotional roadblocks. When my mom saw me, she picked up her purse, walked out the back door, got in her car and drove off. That was a freeing moment for me. I knew right then, it had nothing to do with me. I was free to no longer be a hostage to the most painful experience my life had had. I walked out of their house knowing I wasn't the person my mother made me out to be. Was EVERYTHING resolved and overcome right then? No, those emotional scars are still inside of me, but I took the lesson from that moment, implemented it into my feeling about me and was free to move on. That would have never happened, IF I had not confronted the situation, took what the experience taught me and made the decision *this is my life to live, to design, to experience.*

You will never lose the "wrongs" of yesterday, but

you can turn the "wrong" into a classroom where you can find the lesson that will allow you to start living from Today to Tomorrow! I promise you, *YOU can do that!*

Simple Keys For Letting Go of The Wrongs

K KEEP YOUR SUCCESSES IN SIGHT

E EXPECT THE GOOD, THE BAD AND THE UGLY
   BUT FOCUS ON THE GOOD

Y YESTERDAY BECOMES YOUR LIBRARY OF LESSONS

S STAY CENTERED ON IMPROVING YOUR TALENTS

Chapter 11

Step 6: Enter Every Day Prepared To Have a Simply Great Day!

I know I keep saying this to you, but it is a truth you need to burn into your behavioral thought process – *every day of your life is a choice. It will be what you make it be!*
Is every day going to be the best day ever? NO! But each day you are granted life can be a great day of living. Will a day be without ups and downs? NO! But you can turn lemons into lemonade. It is all about the choice you CHOOSE to make about the events that day hands you.

It is so much fun sitting in airports watching people. I think every type of human God created (and some He may even wonder about) pass through an airport. You have no idea how many experiences I have had that have made me laugh – sometimes out loud.

About four years ago I was traveling from Pittsburgh to New Orleans, and it became one of those traveling days that will try your patience. First, the plane was late, and then, when it did arrive we were informed there was a maintenance issue with the plane.

The young lady at the gate said, "Folks, I am sorry to inform you there is a maintenance issue with the aircraft. The pilot says it is not serious, but we are going to be delayed. If you leave the gate, be sure you are back in about 20 minutes. When the pilot says we can board, we will board. So, don't be gone too long."

With all the years of air travel I knew by the tone of her voice, it was going to be more than 20 minutes. So, I took out my computer and began to work. 20 minutes came and went, the announcement was made about an update coming in another 20 minutes. That 20 minutes came and went.

I couldn't help but watch this gentleman who was growing more and more impatient with each announcement.

Step 6: Enter Every Day Prepared to Have a Simply Great Day!

You could hear him talking to himself. "I can't believe this!" He was talking so loud everyone knew what he was feeling and expressing.

"I always have a problem when I fly with this airline. I promise you I will never fly them again. I can't believe this!"

He stood there staring at the young lady at the counter and continued his out loud personal conversation. "If the issue was not so bad, why is it taking them so long to fix it. I just can't believe this!"

Now, he stopped staring and just started pacing back and forth, and with each circle he made you could sense his frustration growing.

"This is the last thing I needed today! This has to be the worst day of my life."

Almost everyone in the gate area had stopped what they were doing and were watching him. Hey, if you are going to be stuck while they are fixing the plane, why not have some free entertainment, and he was very entertaining!

Finally, he stopped his pacing and took a straight line toward the gate agent. Now, I promise you all eyes were on his journey to the counter.

He got to the counter, slammed his fist on the counter and said in a very loud voice. "What is wrong with you people! If this airplane is broken, just get us another plane. What's so difficult about that?"

The young agent looked at him and calmly said, "Sir, they are working on the situation. I know you have been waiting a while now, but there is nothing I can do. I will let you know when we can board."

Well, that was not what he wanted to hear. With his face turning even redder, his voiced intensified. "I want you to do something about this. Call your supervisor! Hell, call the President of the airlines. Just get me on a plane. Get me out of here!"

You could tell she was loosing her patience with him. "Sir, the plane has a mechanical problem. Would you want to fly on a broken plane? I am doing all I can do. I would appreciate you not yelling at me. I will let you know when the plane is SAFE to fly. Now, would you mind not standing here and talking to me in that tone!"

You have got to know all eyes were on the conversation going on between the two of them. You didn't know whether the gate agent was going to come across the counter and smack him or what. Seeing the look in her eyes, he decided to back off.

I was seated close to where he had been seated before he started his emotional rampage. Coming back over, he paused, looked at me and said, "Can you believe this? Are you on this flight?"

"Yes!"

"Well aren't you upset?"

"No, I'm not, but I think you are upset enough for all of us!"

Whoops! That was the wrong thing to say. Now, his intensity was focused on me. Honestly, I have to tell you I was having a lot of fun with the situation.

Every day of your life is a choice! That is not a statement; it is a fact. On many days you are going to come face to face with the good, the bad and the ugly. Each experience will bring emotions to the surface. What those emotions are and how you deal with them is your choice.

I learned a long time ago, there are not many things

Step 6: Enter Every Day Prepared to Have a Simply Great Day!

worth getting emotionally charged about. There is a solution to everything, but that solution can get lost when the intensity of your emotions grow. As your emotions grow, the dark clouds gather. As they gather, you lose sight of what is really happening. At that point confusion takes over, reaction sets in and life becomes a mess.

Here is something else I have learned. *How you prepare and enter your day can create the day you will have.* Have you ever gotten up on the wrong side of the bed? You know, you got up still being tired, not wanting to do what you were going to have to do today. Your energy was low, you couldn't figure out what to wear, the traffic sucked and the coffee tasted like it was three days old. I mean you just know this was not going to be a good day. When that happens, can if affect your spirit, your emotions, your expectations for the day? You Bet!!

Your day begins with how you get up and approach the day. Your day can be controlled by what you didn't get done yesterday, and you know it is waiting for you when you arrive. When a day starts with your emotions in control, there isn't going to be anything simple about your day.

To **Make Your Life Simply Simple**, you have to start with a day you are prepared for. When you have a purpose for your day, a plan to enact, an agenda you can manage and a commitment to get things done, your day will be a lot simpler. To achieve this you need to start with your mind leading the way. Purpose, plan, agenda and being able to manage your day takes a focused presence.

This is one of the reasons I created my Morning Minute. This is a daily mental preparation program. Each morning you receive a 60 second, 1 minute, video email from me where I share one of my philosophies of life with a brief insight into its meaning for that day. It is yours for one year, 365 days. Go to my website, RichardFlint.com and join the Morning Minute Family.

You have the choice to either prepare for your day or allow your day to manage you. It is your choice, and the more you manage your day the simpler your day becomes.

Simple Keys For Preparing For Your Day

K KEEP FOCUSED ON LIVING FROM TODAY TO TOMORROW

E EXPECT THIS TO BE A DAY OF ACHIEVEMENT

Y YOU ENTER EMOTIONALLY CALM

S START WITH A PURPOSE AND A PLAN

Chapter 11
Conclusion

It's All In Your Hands!

Is it possible to simplify your Life? YES! Is it easy to obtain? NO! It takes a desire that is stronger than the pull of the world around you. Look around your life. How many people do you see whose life is controlled by the drama they wrestle with each day. Is that drama real? For them it is, but does it has to be? My answer is NO!

Your life is going to present you with many different looks. There will be the good, the bad and the ugly. You're going to face each of these in several different forms. Yet, with each experience there is a lesson to be learned, a pathway through the emotional jungle you have to walk through, a road map that will show you the pathway through the ever changing terrain. It is always there waiting on you to take that deep breath, stop reacting and look for the solution that is always present.

Living a life based in making your life simple, demands an everyday commitment to not get caught up in the mess others make of their life. So much of the confusion you will encounter along your journey is the result of you seeking to "fix" someone else's life. Hear me – you can't fix a broken life! Can it be repaired? YES, but you can't fix it!

People come to me on a regular basis and want to know if I can fix their life. I always tell them, "I can't fix what you have done, but I can guide you to face your life, understand how you got here and offer you a process to step out of your mess and move forward."

So many listen, and the expression on their face tells me, "That is not the answer I wanted to hear. I want you to fix it for me."

Whatever your life is, it is YOUR life. No one but YOU can make the changes that will provide YOU with an improved life. It will not happen over night; it will not be as easy as snapping your fingers; it will take YOU desiring it more than fearing what it involves.

You must always remember, *you are emotionally exactly in your life where you want to be.* IF you did not want to be there, you would do whatever it takes to move from living from Yesterday to Today to living from Today to Tomorrow.

It is YOUR life; YOUR life is YOUR design! Living a life that is controlled by confusion or designed with Simplicity is in YOUR HANDS!

The 6 Steps are not magical. They are a process to having the simple life you say you want. The order I gave you is the order you must follow. Change the order, and you will take the *simple* out of *making your life Simply Simple!*

- START WITH FACING WHERE YOUR LIFE IS RIGHT NOW
- INVEST YOUR TIME IN CLEANING UP THE CLUTTER IN YOUR LIFE
- MAKE TIME FOR YOURSELF
- PAUSE WHEN YOU FEEL YOUR LIFE IS BECOMING OVERWHELMED
- LET GO OF THE WRONGS OF YESTERDAY
- ENTER EVERY DAY PREPARED FOR A SIMPLY GREAT DAY

I wish you the best in **Making Your Life Simply Simple!**

Share It With Others

To order copies of this book,
Call 1-800-368-8255
or (757) 873-7722
or visit
www.RichardFlint.com

Special quantity discounts are available
for bulk purchases.

Please allow 2-3 weeks for US delivery.
Canada & International orders

Other Books by Richard Flint

I Need a Life

Behavior Never Lies

Breaking Free

The Truth About Stress

Building Blocks For Strengthening Your Life

Building Blocks For Strengthening Your Relationships

Building Blocks For Improving Customer Relationships

Building Blocks For Controlling Stress

Dictionary of Human Behavior, Volume 1

Dictionary of Human Behavior, Volume 2: Relationships

Dictionary of Human Behavior, Volume 3: Leadership

Quiet Please

Feelings

It Takes A Lot of Pain To Grow Up

Reflections

Sometimes I Really Need To Cry

About The Author

Richard Flint is one of those unique people who has been given the ability to see the clarity in the midst of what looks confusing. Since 1980, he has been sharing his insights and philosophies with audiences all over the world. He is known as the person who knows you even though he has never met you. He has written 17 books, recorded over 60 cds, and filmed 30 dvds. Beyond being an author, he is a nationally recognized speaker, a lifestyle coach to many who are seeking to stop repeating and start achieving, and host of his own internet radio and web-tv shows. But more than all this, you will find him to be a friend whose understandings can calm your emotional confusion.

www.RichardFlint.com

SERVICES AVAILABLE

On-site training, consulting and keynote speaking. *It's simple.* Richard Flint can make your people better. He can customize any of his programs and come right to your company's door. He also provides a full range of in-house consulting services, and is always delighted to add sparkle to your next corporate or association meeting with a stimulating keynote presentation designed just for you.

For more information about Richard's on-site services, call our Marketing Department at 1-800-368-8255.

Whether you have 30 or 3,000 people to make better, Richard Flint is the answer.

www.RichardFlint.com

It's Time To Take Your Life To The Next Dimension!

The Power To Be!

A 12-part subscription series dealing with the 12 biggest hurdles you face in your success journey!

Powerful 12 Part Online Training Series!
$39.95
per month

Monthly Subscription Includes:

- Monthly On-Line Training Video
- Downloadable MP3 Audio File
- Downloadable PDF Program Study Guide
- 3-ring custom binder to organize materials
- PLUS a FREE CD Program each month to compliment the training (a $69 value!)

12-Part Monthly Subscription is 12 monthly payments of $39.95 AFTER 30-Day FREE Trial Bonus Program

~ OR ~

BEST VALUE! Purchase the <u>Entire</u> Series for just $429.97 (Save $49.43) That's a program every month for 13 months!

Get Started Today at www.RichardFlint.com